The Secret Rose Garden

By

Mahmud Shabistari

Translated by

Florence Lederer

First published in 1920

Published by Left of Brain Books

Copyright © 2023 Left of Brain Books

ISBN 978-1-396-32660-8

First Edition

All rights reserved. No part of this publication may be reproduced, distributed, or transmitted in any form or by any means, including photocopying, recording, or other electronic or mechanical methods, without the prior written permission of the publisher, except in the case of brief quotations permitted by copyright law. Left of Brain Books is a division of Left Of Brain Onboarding Pty Ltd.

PUBLISHER'S PREFACE

About the Book

"The Secret Rose Garden of Sa'd Ud Din Mahmud Shabistari, Translated by Florence Lederer."

(Quote from sacred-texts.com)

About the Author

Mahmud Shabistari (1288 - 1320)

"Mahmud Shabistari (1288 - 1320s) is one of the most celebrated Persian Sufi poets of the 14th century. He was born in Tabriz in 1288 (687 AH), where he received his education. He became deeply versed in the symbolic terminology of Ibn Arabi. He wrote during a period of Mongol invasions. His most famous work is a mystic text called "The Secret Rose Garden" (Gulshan-i Raz) written about 1311 in rhyming couplets (Mathnawi). This poem was written in response to twenty six queries concerning Sufi metaphysics posed to him by the great Rukh Al Din Amir Husayn Harawi (d. 1318). It was also the main reference used by Francois Bernier when explaining Sufism to his European friends (in: Lettre sur le Quietisme des Indes; 1688). He died in 1320-1321 [AD]."

(Quote from wikipedia.org)

CONTENTS

PUBLISHER'S PREFACE
EDITORIAL NOTE 1
INTRODUCTION 2
ACKNOWLEDGMENT 14
    THE PERFECT FACE OF THE BELOVED 15
    BEAUTY 20
    THE SEA AND ITS PEARLS 22
    THE JOURNEY 24
    TIME AND THIS DREAM-WORLD 29
    REFLECTIONS 32
    DIVINE INEBRIATION 35
    REASON AND FREE-WILL 39
    MAN: HIS CAPABILITIES AND HIS DESTINY 42
    THE ONE 47
    THE SELF 50
    IDOLS, GIRDLES, AND CHRISTIANITY 51
    THOUGHTS 54
    THE LIGHT MANIFEST 59
EPILOGUE 62

EDITORIAL NOTE

THE object of the Editors of this series is a very definite one. They desire above all things that, in their humble way, these books shall be the ambassadors of good-will and understanding between East and West--the old world of Thought and the new of Action. In this endeavour, and in their own sphere, they are but followers of the highest example in the land. They are confident that a deeper knowledge of the great ideals and lofty philosophy of Oriental thought may help to a revival of that true spirit of Charity which neither despises nor fears the nations of another creed and colour.

L. CRANMER-BYNG.
S. A. KAPADIA.

INTRODUCTION

LIFE OF SHABISTARĪ

"It is inward glow that makes the Sūfī, not the religious habit."

SA'D UD DIN MAHMŪD SHABISTARĪ was born at Shabistar, near Tabriz, about A.D. 1250.

He wrote the Gulshan i Rāz, or Secret Rose Garden, as a reply to questions put forth by a Sūfī doctor of Herat named Dmir Syad Hosaini.

Very little is known of Mahmūd Shabistarī's life. He wrote beside the Gulshan i Rāz two treatises on Sūfiism called Hakk ul Yakin and Risala i Shadīd.

We learn he had a very favourite disciple called Shaikh Ibrahim.

The Gulshan i Rāz was introduced into Europe by two travellers in 1700. Later, copies of the poem were found in several European libraries.

In 1821 Dr. Tholuck, of Berlin, published extracts, and in 1825 a German translation of part of the poem appeared in another of his books. Afterwards a verse translation and the Persian text was published by Von Hammer Purgstall in Berlin and Vienna.

The Gulshan i Rāz was translated into English and published, with the Persian text and extracts from Hammer's edition and Lajihi's notes, by Mr. Whinfield in 1880.

SŪFĪ POETRY

Readers of Sūfī poetry for the first time are liable to be amazed, perhaps even repelled, by the extravagant language, by the familiarity with the Deity, by the apparent disregard of all human and Divine laws. But on further examination the wonder of the Sūfīs' love for their Beloved shines out with a clear intensity, a beautiful luminous brightness.

They are in love with The One, and their love takes the form of exquisite songs of praise and wonder:

"I heard entranced; my spirit rushed to meet
Love's welcome order, for the voice was sweet."

Vaughan says:

"Oriental mysticism has become famous by its poets, and into poetry it has thrown all its force and fire."

"The Sūfīs . . . have one sole and simple task, to make

Their hearts a stainless mirror for their God."
Love is the Sūfīs' theme, Divine, Eternal Love, and into this sea of Love they cast themselves headlong.

Rūmī sings:

"Moths, burnt by the torch of the Beloved's face,
Are the lovers who linger in the sanctuary."

"If we are called madmen or drunkards,
'Tis because of the Cupbearer and the Cup."

"Because my mouth has eaten of His sweetmeats
In a clear vision I can see Him face to face."

SŪFĪ SYMBOLISM

In reading the enraptured poetry of the Sūfīs, it should be borne in mind that, though the symbols of earthly love and beauty are freely used, yet the real meaning is concealed. No doubt this was originally done to keep secret their mystic love, lest the profane should scoff. But as time went on certain words began to have a recognized meaning amongst themselves. For instance:

EMBRACES and KISSES are raptures of love.

SLEEP is contemplation, PERFUME the wish for Divine favour.

IDOLATERS mean men of the pure faith, not infidels.

WINE, which was forbidden by Mahomet to his followers, was used as a word-symbol by the Sūfīs to denote spiritual knowledge, and the WINE-SELLER means the spiritual guide.

A TAVERN is a place where the wine of Divine love inebriates the pilgrim.

INTOXICATION means religious ecstasy, MIRTH the joy in the love of the Deity.

BEAUTY means the glory of the Beloved.

CURLS and TRESSES mean plurality veiling the face of Unity from its lovers.

The CHEEK means Divine essence of names and qualities.

The DOWN is the world of pure spirits which is nearest to Divinity.

The MOLE on the cheek is the point of indivisible Unity.

The TORCH is the light kindled in the heart by the Beloved.

We thus see that to the Sūfī the love between man and woman is a shadowed picture of the love between the soul and God, and just as a lover will dream of his beloved, singing her praises, and thirsting for a sight of her face, so do the Sūfīs eternally dream of their God, ever contemplating His attributes, and consumed with a burning desire for His presence.

The history of mysticism contains many impassioned love songs to the Absolute, but in Sūfī poetry there is a peculiar richness, a depth, a colour which fascinates and charms so many of us.

Sūfī poetry abounds in allegories and love romances, the stories of Laylā and Majnūm, Yūsuf and Zulaikā, Salāmān and Absāl, in which it is easy to read the hidden meaning of passion for the Absolute. Various are the love themes of the Sūfīs; we hear songs of: the nightingale in love with the rose, the moth fluttering round the light of the candle, the moaning dove who has lost her mate, the snow melting in the desert and mounting as vapour to the sky, of a dark night in the desert through which a frenzied camel madly plunges, of a reed torn from its bed and made into a flute whose plaintive music fills the eyes with tears. [1]

---

[1] See R. A. Nicholson's Mystics of Islam, p. 117.

THE BELOVED

The Sūfīs' conception of the Beloved is essentially personal, though there is nothing to show that they worshipped Him as a person, or assigned to Him a form.

Being pantheists, they probably believed that He was the One Light shining in myriad forms through the whole universe, One essence remaining the same.

"Every moment the robber Beauty rises in a different shape, ravishes the soul and disappears.
Every instant the Loved One assumes a new garment, now of old, now of youth.
Now He plunged into the heart of the substance of the potter's clay--the Spirit plunged like a diver.
Anon He rose from the depths of mud that is moulded and baked,
Then he appeared in the world." [1]

And Jāmī declares:

"In neighbour, friend, companion, Him we see,
In beggar's rags or robes of royalty,
In Union's cell or in distraction haunts,
There's none but He, by God, there's none but He." [2]

The Sūfīs realized that it is impossible in spatial terms to describe that which is even beyond pure spirit.

Plotinus has told us in a beautiful passage that a

---

[1] Mystics of Islam, R. A. Nicholson.
[2] Jāmī's Lawa'ih, translated by E. H. Whinfield.

"We must not be surprised that that which excites the keenest of longings is without any form, even spiritual form, since the soul itself, when inflamed with love for it, puts off all the form which it had, even that which belongs to the spiritual world." [1]

The inability to describe to the uninitiated the secret love of the mystic for the Unknowable is made the subject of an exquisite poem by the Indian poet Tagore:

"I boasted among men that I had known you. They see your picture in all works of mine. They come and ask me who is he? I know not how to answer them. I say, 'Indeed, I cannot tell.' They blame me and they go away in scorn. And you sit there smiling. I put my tales of you into lasting songs. The secret gushes out from my heart. They come and ask me, 'Tell me all your meaning.' I know not how to answer them. I say, 'Ah, who knows what they mean.' They smile and go away in utter scorn. And you sit there smiling." [2]

FROM THE UNREAL TO THE REAL

The Sūfīs believed that the phenomenal world is the Unreal, that the reason men are blind to the existence of the Real world, which is the Spiritual, is because there are veils and mists separating the soul from God.

This world appears Real to the man who cannot use his spiritual eye and view the Beyond. Having no discernment of the Unseen, he does not believe in its existence.

---

[1] Philosophy of Plotinus, by Dean Inge.
[2] Gitanjali, by Rabindranath Tagore.

But whosoever becomes aware of the Divine Light shining in the heart, and who realises the love of God in the soul, is able to pass from the Unreal to the Real; he will see:

"Gold wherever we go, and pearls
Wherever we turn, and silver in the waste."

So exquisite is the vision of the All-Beautiful that whoever has had this vision instantly becomes enamoured, and leaves the world of shadows and change to contemplate the One.

He will not rest until he has purified his life, cast aside everything that may be a hindrance in his path, and he will spend his whole life in communion with God, at the same time pouring out in love-songs and praise all the worship and adoration of his soul.

"By God, sun never rose or set but Thou wert
My heart's desire and my dream.
And I never sat conversing with any people
But Thou wert the subject of my conversation
In the midst of my comrades.
And I never mentioned Thee in joy or sorrow
But love for Thee was mingled with my breath.
And I never resolved to drink water, when I was athirst,
But I saw an image of Thee in the cup.
And were I able to come I would have visited Thee,
Crawling on my face or walking on my head."

When the Sūfī has passed to the Real World he is able to see earthly existence in its true light:
"I am lost to myself and unconscious,
And my attributes are annihilated.
To-day I am lost to all things:
Naught remains but a forced expression."

Passing through a world of shadows he fixes his eye on Eternity; the happenings of the universe appear to him unworthy of exultation, grief, or sorrow.

Earthly love seems worthless, insipid, and dull, compared to his flaming devotion for the Unchangeable.
He has one desire, one aim, one goal--to reach the bliss which he has briefly touched in rare moments of ecstasy and rapture.

To find the far-off mystic city which

"Mystery shrouds . . . now from mortal eyes,
Save when upon some lone lost wanderer's sight
Its diamond turrets like a day-dream rise."

THE ART OF SHABISTARĪ

I have already said that little is known of Shabistarī's life, but of his learning and knowledge of Sūfiism there is ample evidence in this book; and though he does not charm with the subtle fascination of Hafiz, though he has not the originality of Rūmī or in style cannot compare with the elegance of Jāmī, yet in plainness and directness of speech, and in earnestness of purpose, he perhaps outweighs them all. He gives us a clear, bright vision in brilliant sunshine of Virtue and Vice, Reality and Illusion, Wisdom and Ignorance.

We do not find ourselves in the twilight of a faintly-coloured land where we sometimes wander, drawn hither by the sweet voices of the Sūfīs, where, midst the delicate perfumes of an Oriental garden, the lover is singing entrancing love-songs, whether of earthly passion or of Divine intoxication remains a matter of heated controversy to this day.

Neither are we given such daring advice as Jāmī gives when he sings:

"Drink deep of earthly love, that so thy lip

May learn the wine of holier love to sip."

Mahmūd's vision of Reality was direct and distinct, not the oblique view which is the vision of some mystics, and from this Reality he is able to distinguish sharply between the conflicting forces of Good and Evil.

He makes a passionate appeal to humanity to seek for the Truth, to desire the substance and not the mirage, to ignore the allurement and illusion of earthly love, and instead to centre on the Beloved all the heart's adoration.

THE SECRET ROSE GARDEN

It is nearly seven hundred years since Mahmūd planted his garden with roses of Love and Adoration, of Reason and of spiritual Illumination. Since then many have wandered there, lingering in the secret paths and plucking the scented

blossoms to carry back into the world of shadows and unreality. What is the fadeless colour of these Roses? What is their lasting grace of form, and what perfumed attar from them lingers on through the ages?

The poem opens with the statement of the sole existence of the One Real Being, and of the illusion of this world's mirage. How is man to reach knowledge of God? By thought, for--

"Thought is passing from the false to the true."
But reason and sense cannot throw off the apparent reality of the phenomenal world. Reason looking at the Light of Lights is blinded like a bat by the sun. It is then a consciousness arises in the soul of its own nothingness. At this point (annihilation of the self) it is possible for man to discern the light of the Spirit. In this world are mirrored the various attributes of Being, and each atom of Not-Being reflects some one Divine attribute:

"Each atom hides beneath its veil
The soul-amazing beauty of the Beloved's face."

And these atoms are ever longing to rejoin their source.

The journey to the Beloved has only two stages: dying to self and uniting with the Truth.

When man's lower self is dead, the real self remains and is above the dominion of the law.

These two stages--the "journey to God" and the "journey down to God"--are a circuit. He who has revolved round this circuit is a perfect man.

On being born into this world man is possessed by evil passions, and if he gives way to them his soul is lost. But in each soul there is an instinct for God and a longing for holiness. If man will foster this instinct and develop this longing, a Divine light will shine on him, and he, repenting, turns and journeys towards God; casting away self, he will meet and be united with the Truth in spirit.

This is the holy state of the saints and prophets.

But the man must not rest in this Divine union. He must return to this world of unreality, and in the downward journey must keep the ordinary laws and creeds of men.

This phenomenal existence, i.e. Not-being, is an illusion which is typified by considering the unreality of echoes and reflections and by pondering on past and future time, and on passing events, which seem at the moment of their existence to be real, but fading into the past become vague and shadowy.

The dispositions acquired by man in this life will in the next world be manifested in spiritual bodies; each form will be appropriate to its past life. The material idea of Paradise and houris will then be known to be an idle tale. No quality or distinction will remain for the perfect will. Then drink of the cup of union with God.

Such is the hope of the Sūfīs, but in this world the intoxication of the cup of union is followed by the headache of separation.

THE CENTRAL TREE OF BEAUTY

All round his garden Mahmūd has planted these roses of Reason, Belief, Knowledge, and Faith; they are blooming everywhere, beautiful in their vivid colouring of Truth and Purity. But it is in the centre that we find a Rose-tree of glory unequalled, glowing with the blossoms of love's devotion; this is the tree which Mahmūd planted with all his heart's adoration-- the description of the perfect face of the Beloved.

It is at this spot we wait entranced, and through the mystic stillness we seem to hear the voice of him who, long ago for love's sake, planted this Rose-tree, echoing his sublime utterance:

"See but One, say but One, know but One."

FLORENCE LEDERER.

ACKNOWLEDGMENT

I wish to acknowledge my indebtedness to Professor E. H. Whinfield, whose book, the standard translation of the Gulshan i Rāz, has been of the greatest assistance to me in compiling this little volume. I am grateful to Dr. R. A. Nicholson for kind permission to quote from his works on Sūfiism, and to Captain L. Cranmer-Byng I offer my best thanks for his kind interest in my work, and for many helpful hints and suggestions.

THE PERFECT FACE OF THE BELOVED

THE EYE AND THE LIP

WHAT is the nature of the eye and the lip?
Let us consider.

Coquettish and intoxicating glances shine from His eye.
The essence of existence issues from His ruby lip.
Hearts burn with desire because of His eye,
And are healed again by the smile of His lip.

Because of His eye hearts are aching and drunken.
His ruby lip gives soul-garments to men.
His eye does not perceive this visible world,
Yet often His lip quivers with compassion.

Sometimes He charms us with a touch of humanity,
And gives help to the despairing.
It is His smile that gives life to man's water and clay;
It is His breath that opens heaven's gate for us.
A corn-baited snare is each glance of that eye,

And a wine-shop lurks in each corner.
When He frowns the wide world is laid waste,
But is restored every moment by His kiss.
Our blood is at fever point because of His eye,
Our souls demented because of His lip.

How He has despoiled our hearts by a frown!
How He has uplifted our souls by a smile!

If you ask of Him an embrace,
His eye will say "Yea," His lip "Nay."
He finished the creation of the world by a frown,
Now and then the soul is revived by a kiss.
We would give up our lives with despair at His frown,
But would rise from the dead at his kiss.

. . . When the world meditates on His eye and His lip,
It yields itself to the intoxication of wine.

THE MOLE

THE single point of the mole in His cheek
Is a centre from which circles
A circumference.
The two worlds circle round that centre.
The heart and soul of Adam evolved from there.

. . . Hearts bleed because they are a reflection
Of the point of that black mole,
And both are stagnant; for there is no escape
Of the reflection from the reflect.

Unity will not embrace Plurality,
For the point of Unity has one root only.
. . . I wonder if His mole is the reflection of my heart,
Or my heart the reflection of His mole.
Was my heart created from His mole's reflection?
Or may it be seen shining in His mole?
I wonder if my heart is in His face,
Or if His mole abides in my heart.
But this is a deep secret hidden, alas! from me.

. . . If my heart is a reflection,
Why is it ever so changing?

Sometimes tired like His brilliant eye,
Sometimes waving to and fro as His curl waves,
Sometimes a shining moonbeam like His face,
Sometimes a dark shadow like His mole,
Sometimes it is a mosque, sometimes a synagogue,
Sometimes a hell, sometimes a heaven,
Sometimes soaring above the seventh heaven,
Sometimes buried far below this earth.

. . . After a spell the devotee and ascetic
Turns again to wine, lamp, and beauty.

THE CURL

IF you ask of me the long story
Of the Beloved's curl,
I cannot answer, for it contains a mystery
Which only true lovers understand,
And they, maddened by its beauty,
Are held captive as by a golden chain.
I spoke too openly of that graceful form,
But the end of the curl told me to hide its glory,
So that the path to it should be twisted
And crooked and difficult.

That curl enchains lovers' hearts,
And bears their souls to and fro
In the sea of desire. A hundred thousand hearts
Are tightly bound, not one escapes, alas!

No single infidel would remain in the world
If he could see the shaking aside
Of those black curls,

And on the earth there would not remain a faithful soul
If they were always in their place.
Suppose they were shorn. . . . No matter,
Day would increase and the night disappear.

As a spider spreads its nets to ensnare,
So does the Beloved in wantonness
Shake His locks from off His face.

Behold His hands plundering Reason's caravan
And with knots binding it tight.

Never at rest is that curl,
Ever moving to and fro
Making now night, making now morning,
Playing with the seasons in wonder.

Adam was created when the perfume of that
amber-scented curl
Was blown by the wind on his clay.

And I too possess an ensample;
I cannot wait for a moment,
But breathlessly start working anew
To tear my heart out of my breast.
. . . Sore troubled am I by that curl
Which veils my longing soul from His face.

THE CHEEK AND THE DOWN

THE theatre of Divine beauty is the cheek,
And the down is the entrance to His holy presence.
Beauty is erased by His cheek, who says,
"Without my presence you are non-existent."
In the unseen world the down is as green meadows

Leading to the mansion of Eternal Life.
The blackness of His curl turns day into night,
The down of His cheek holds the secret of life.
If only you can glimpse His face and its down,
You will understand the meaning of plurality and unity.
His curl will teach you the knowledge of this world,
His down will reveal hidden paths.

Imagine seven verses in which each letter
Contains oceans of mysteries;
Such is His cheek.
And imagine, hidden beneath each hair of His cheek,
Thousands of oceans of mysteries;
Such is His down.

As the heart is God's throne in the water,
So is the down the ornament of the soul.

BEAUTY

THE MARRIAGE OF THE SOUL

DESCENDING to the earth,
That strange intoxicating beauty of the unseen world
Lurks in the elements of Nature.

And the soul of man,
Who has attained the rightful balance,
Becoming aware of this hidden joy,
Straightway is enamoured and bewitched.

And from this mystic marriage are born
The poets' songs, inner knowledge,
The language of the heart, virtuous living,
And the fair child Beauty.

And the Great Soul gives to man as dowry
The hidden glory of the world.

THE CHARM OF BEAUTY

FROM the unseen world descends
Heavenly beauty,
And plants its flag in the city
Of earthly fairness,
Throwing the world's array into confusion;
Now riding the steed of comeliness,
Now flourishing the sword of eloquence,
And all alike bow down,

Saints and kings, dervishes and prophets,
Swayed by the charm of Beauty's fascination.

EARTHLY BEAUTY

WHENCE the charm of a fair face?
Not earthly beauty only
Can so allure us with its loveliness.
Perchance we see in this, as in a cloudy mirror,
The far faint reflect of the Perfect Face.
And these deep feelings of delight and wonder
Can only issue from the One True Beauty,
For in Divine Perfection there is no other partner.
Nor is it all desire and lust that tempts men's hearts with longing.
. . . Evil appears but as the other side of Truth.

THE SEA AND ITS PEARLS

A DROP OF SEA-WATER

BEHOLD how this drop of sea-water
Has taken so many forms and names;
It has existed as mist, cloud, rain, dew, and mud,
Then plant, animal, and perfect man;
And yet it was a drop of water
From which these things appeared.
Even so this universe of reason, soul, heavens, and bodies,
Was but a drop of water in its beginning and ending.

. . . When a wave strikes it, the world vanishes;
And when the appointed time comes to heaven and stars,
Their being is lost in not being.

THE SEA OF BEING

IN Being's silver sea
Lustrous pearls of knowledge are washed up
On the shore of speech,
And dainty shells bring poems in their curving forms
To strew the beach with beauty.

Each wave that breaks in foaming arcs
Casts up a thousand royal pearls
That hold strange murmuring voices,
Gems of devotion, joy, and love.
Yet though a thousand waves
At every moment rise and fall,

Scattering pearls and shells,

Yet are there ever more and more to come,
Nor is that sea of Being less by one sheer drop.

PEARLS OF KNOWLEDGE

IN the sea of 'Uman, the pearl oysters
Rise to the surface from the lowest depths,
And wait with opened mouths.
Then arises from the sea a mist,

Which falls again in raindrops
Into the mouths of the shells
(At the command of the Truth).
Straightway is each closed as by a hundred bonds,
And the shells sink back again
Into the ocean's depths,
Bearing in their hearts the pearl drops
Which the divers seek and find.
The sea is Being, the shore the body;
The mist, grace, and the rain, knowledge of the Name;
Human Wisdom is the diver
Who holds enwrapped in his garment
A hundred pearls;
The soul in a swift lightning's flash
Bears to the listening ear voices and messages
From the shells of knowledge;
Then when the husks are opened,
Behold the royal shimmering pearls!

THE JOURNEY

THE FORSAKING

SEE, your companions have gone;
Will you not too make a start?
If you desire to take wing as a bird,
Then leave to the vultures this carrion world.

Forsake your relations,
For your real Friend must be sought.
He who is drowning in the sea of Not-being
Must cast aside all relationships.
What are father and mother,
Sister and brother?
Your very son may be your enemy,
Yet may a stranger be your kinsman;
Even your fellow-travellers on the mystic path
Must be renounced.

All relations are a bond, a spell,
A fairy dream,
An absolute illusion.

Omit not the duties
Of the law to them,
But have regard to yourself.
. . . Abandon gold and women,
For they are a source of anxiety.

THE TRAVELLER

THE traveller on the path,
'Tis he who knows from whence he cometh;
Then doth he journey hastily,
Becoming as pure from self as fire from smoke.
Unfolded to him are a series of revelations
From the beginning. Till he is led away
From darkness and sin.
He now retraces stage by stage his steps
Till he reaches his goal the Perfect.
Thus is the perfect man evolved
From the time he first exists
As inorganic matter,
Next a breath of spirit, and he is living

And from God draws his motive powers.
Next the Truth makes him lord of his will,
As in childhood his discernment of the world unfolds.
And now the world's temptations assail him.

. . . Anger appears and desires of the flesh,
And then avarice, pride, and gluttony;
His nature becomes evil,
Worse than an animal or demon;
Now is he at the lowest point of all,
The point opposite to Unity.
. . . Should he remain fettered in this snare,
He goes further astray than the beasts;
But if there shines a light from the spirit world,
Divinely attractive,
Or if he can find a reflection of proof,
Then will his heart respond in a feeling of kinship
To this Light of the Truth,
And he will turn back and retrace his steps

From whence he came.
To faith assured he has found his way
Through certain proof, or the wonder
And attraction of the Divine,

. . . He throws away his selfhood utterly
And ascends in the steps of the most Pure.

EXHORTATION

THOUGH the world is yours, you remain dejected,
Who so pitiable as you?

You, who are a man, arise and pass on,
Wait not day or night at the halting-stages,
Tarry not behind your fellow-travellers and the caravans.

THE TWO STEPS OF THE JOURNEY

THE journey of the pilgrims is two steps and no more:
One is the passing out of selfhood,
And one towards mystical Union with the Friend.

FEAR

As the Arab racer needs not the whip,
So you will not need to fear
When on your journey you have started.

When purified are your soul and body,
You will not fear the fires of hell.
Throw pure gold into the fire;
If it contains no alloy, what is there to burn?

LOGIC

IF God guides you not into the road,
It will not be disclosed by logic.

Logic is a bondage of forms;
A road that is long and hard.
Leave it for a season. Like Moses
Cast away that staff
And enter for awhile "The Valley of Peace."

THE INFANT AND THE YOUTH

THE young infant in the cradle
Stays at his mother's side,
But when he is grown manly
He goes forth with his father.

So you remain with your mother,
The fleshly elements,
Until you join your Father up on high.

THE ALMOND-TREE

As the kernel of an almond is spoilt utterly
If it is plucked from its husk while unripe,
So error in the path of the pilgrim
Spoils the kernel of his soul.
When the knower is divinely illumined,
The kernel ripens, bursts the husk,
And departs, returning no more.
But another retains the husk,
Though shining as a. bright sun,
And makes another circuit.
From water and earth springs up into a tree,

Whose high branches are lifted up to heaven;
Then from the seed of this tree
A hundredfold are brought forth.
Like the growth of a seed into the line of a tree,
From point comes a line, then a circle;
When the circuit of this circle is complete,
Then the last is joined to the first.

INTERMINGLING

You are plurality transformed into Unity,
And Unity passing into plurality;
This mystery is understood when man
Leaves the part and merges in the Whole.

TIME AND THIS DREAM-WORLD

TIME

THE past has flown away,
The coming month and year do not exist;
Ours only is the present's tiny point.

Time is but a fancied dot ever moving on
Which you have called a flowing river-stream.

I am alone in a wide desert,
Listening to the echo of strange noises.

THE DREAM OF LIFE

You have heard much of this world,
Yet what have you seen of this world?
What is its form and substance?
What is Simurgh, and what is Mount Kaf?
What is Hades and what is Heaven and Hell?
What is that unseen world
A day of which equals a year of this?

Come and hear the meaning.

You are asleep, and your vision is a dream,
All you are seeing is a mirage.
When you wake up on the morn of the last day
You will know all this to be Fancy's illusion;
When you have ceased to see double,

Earth and Heaven will become transformed;
When the real sun unveils his face to you,
The moon, the stars, and Venus will disappear;
If a ray shines on the hard rock
Like wool of many colours, it drops to pieces.

THE PHENOMENAL WORLD

THE world is an imaginary figure,
A diffused shadow of the Infinite;
One breath created the worlds of command
And all living things.

As they appear to come forth, so they appear to go.
Though there is no real coming and going.
For what is going but coming?

. . . All are one, both the visible and the invisible.
God most high, the Eternal One,
Creates and destroys both worlds.

. . . The varied forms you see are but phantoms of your fancy,
And by revolving quickly in a circle
Appear as one.

THE REAL AND THE UNREAL

THE imagination produces phenomenal objects
Which have no real existence,
So this world has no substantial reality,
But exists as a shadowy pageant or a play.

All is pervaded by Absolute Being

In its utter perfection.

There are many numbers, but only One is counted.

THIS WORLD A MIRAGE

THE house is left empty, save for the Truth,
For in a moment the world has passed away;
Then you, rid of self, fly upwards

And are united to the Beloved.
Union is yours when this dream-world
Fades and dies away.

REFLECTIONS

SUN-REFLECTIONS

SUN-REFLECTIONS from the unseen world
Are all the objects of this mortal sphere,
As curl, down, mole, and brow on a fair face.
For Beauty absolute reigns over all.

. . . When the ears first hear these words
They seem to denote sensual objects.
But as there is no language for the Infinite,
How can we express its mysteries
In finite words?
Or how can the visions of the ecstatic
Be described in earthly formula?
So mystics veil their meanings
In these shadows of the unseen,
The objects of the senses.

. . . As a nurse to an infant,
So is the Infinite to the finite.

. . . Once these words were used in their proper sense,
But now are concealed lest the vulgar should profane.

Annihilation, intoxication, the fever of love
Are the three states of the mystic,
And those who abide in these states
At once comprehend the meanings
Veiled in the words.

But if you know them not,
Pretend not you understand like an ignorant infidel,
For all cannot be mystics or grasp the mysteries.
No mere illusions are the mystic's dreams,
And a man of truth does not vainly talk.
To comprehend requires revelations or great faith.

Briefly have I explained these words and their meanings
So that you may apply them in their right intent,
Remembering the attributes of each.
Compare them in a right manner,
And refrain from the wrong comparisons.

Now that these rules are understood
I will show you more of their application.

THE MIRROR

YOUR eye has not strength enough
To gaze at the burning sun,
But you can see its brilliant light
By watching its reflection
Mirrored in the water.

So the reflection of Absolute Being
Can be viewed in this mirror of Not-Being,
For non-existence, being opposite Reality,
Instantly catches its reflection.

Know the world from end to end is a mirror;
In each atom a hundred suns are concealed.
If you pierce the heart of a single drop of water,
From it will flow a hundred clear oceans;
If you look intently at each speck of dust,

In it you will see a thousand beings,
A gnat in its limbs is like an elephant;
In name a drop of water resembles the Nile,
In the heart of a barley-corn is stored an hundred harvests,
Within a millet-seed a world exists,
In an insect's wing is an ocean of life,

A heaven is concealed in the pupil of an eye,
The core in the centre of the heart is small,
Yet the Lord of both worlds will enter there.

EVIL

BLACKEN the back of a mirror
And it will reflect your face,
So the dust of the earth reflects
The rays of the sun in the seventh heaven.

THE REFLECTION IN THE MIRROR

HOLD up a mirror before you
And gaze on that other person.
. . . Again look and consider;
Your proper self is here, not there.
What, then, can be this reflection,
This shadow of your face?

In the same way as light and dark are not connected,
Being is not joined to Not-Being.

DIVINE INEBRIATION

TAVERN-HAUNTERS

THE tavern is the abode of lovers,
The place where the bird of the soul nests,
The rest-house that has no existence
In a world that has no form.
The tavern-haunter is desolate in a lonely desert,
Where he sees the world as a mirage.
The desert is limitless and endless,
For no man has seen its beginning or ending.
Though you feverishly wander for a hundred years
You will be always alone.
For the dwellers there are headless and footless,
Neither the faithful nor infidels,
They have renounced both good and evil,
And have cast away name and fame,
From drinking the cup of selflessness;

Without lips or mouth,
And are beyond traditions, visions, and states,
Beyond dreaming of secret rooms, of lights and miracles.

They are lying drunken through the smell of the wine-dregs,
And have given as ransom
Pilgrim's staff and cruse,
Dentifrice and rosary.

Sometimes rising to the world of bliss,
With necks exalted as racers,

Or with blackened faces turned to the wall,
Sometimes with reddened faces tied to the stake.
Now in the mystic dance of joy in the Beloved,
Losing head and foot like the revolving heavens.
In every strain which they hear from the minstrel
Comes to them rapture from the unseen world.

For within the mere words and sounds
Of the mystic song
Lies a precious mystery.

From drinking one cup of the pure wine,
From sweeping the dust of dung-hills from their souls,
From grasping the skirts of drunkards,
They have become Sūfīs.

THE WINE OF RAPTURE

THE wine, lit by a ray from his face,
Reveals the bubbles of form,
Such as the material world and the soul-world,
Which appear as veils to the saints.
Universal Reason seeing this is astounded,
Universal Soul is reduced to servitude.

Drink wine! for the bowl is the face of the Friend.
Drink wine! for the cup is his eye, drunken and flown with wine.
Drink wine! and be free from heart-coldness,
For a drunkard is better than the self-satisfied.

The whole world is his tavern,
His wine-cup the heart of each atom,
Reason is drunken, angels drunken, soul drunken,
Air drunken, earth drunken, heaven drunken.
The sky, dizzy from the wine-fumes' aroma,

Is staggering to and fro;
The angels, sipping pure wine from goblets,
Pour down the dregs on the world;
From the scent of these dregs man rises to heaven.
Inebriated from the draught, the elements
Fall into water and fire.
Catching the reflection, the frail body becomes a soul,
And the frozen soul by its heat
Thaws and becomes living.
The creature world remains giddy,
For ever straying from house and home.

One from the dregs' odour becomes a philosopher,
One viewing the wine's colour becomes a relater,
One from half a draught becomes religious,
One from a bowlful becomes a lover,
Another swallows at one draught
Goblet, tavern, cup-bearer, and drunkards;
He swallows all, but still his mouth stays open.

WINE, TORCH, AND BEAUTY

TRUTH'S manifestations
Are wine, torch, and beauty;
Wine and torch are the light and shining of the "knower,"
Beauty is concealed from none.
Wine is the lamp-shade,
And torch the lamp;
Beauty is the Spirit-light,
So bright, it kindles sparks
In the heart.
Wine and torch are the essence of that blinding light,
Beauty is the sign of the Divine.

Drink this wine and, dying to self,
You will be freed from the spell of self.
Then will your being, as a drop,
Fall into the ocean of the Eternal.

INTOXICATION

WHAT is pure wine?
It is self-purification.
What sweetness! what intoxication! what blissful ecstasy!

Oh! happy moment when ourselves we quit,
When fallen in the dust, drunken and amazed,
In utter poverty we shall be rich and free.
Of what use then will be paradise and houris?
For no alien can find entrance to that mystic room.

I know not what will happen after
I have seen this vision and imbibed this cup,
But after all intoxication comes headache,
Anguish drowns my soul remembering this!

REASON AND FREE-WILL

REASON

LET reason go. For his light
Burns reason up from head to foot.
If you wish to see that Face,
Seek another eye. The philosopher
With his two eyes sees double,
So is unable to see the unity of the Truth.
As his light burns up the angels,
Even so doth it consume reason.
As the light of our eyes to the sun,
So is the light of reason to the Light of Lights.

KNOWLEDGE

LEARNING is only the outer wrapping
Of the letter;
The dry husk that covers the nut,
Not the kernel concealed within;

Yet must the husk exist
To ripen the kernel.
So from learning comes the sweet knowledge of Faith.
Oh! soul of my brother, hearken,
Strive to gain knowledge of faith,
For the "knower" in both worlds
Has a high place.
Knowledge loves not this world of form
Which is void of Reality.

Begin to till your field
For next year's harvest.
Knowledge is your heritage,
Be adorned with the principle of all virtues.

THE BLINDNESS OF REASON

As the man blind from his birth
Believes not nor understands
Your description of colours,
Even if you show him proofs for a century,
So blind reason cannot see the future state.

But beyond reason man has a certain knowledge
Which God has placed in his soul and body
Whereby he perceives hidden mysteries.
And like the fire in flint and steel
When these are struck together,
The two worlds for him are lit up in a flash.

FREE-WILL

You say, "I myself have Free-will,
For my body is the horse and my soul the rider,
The reins of the body are in the hands of the soul,
The entire direction is given to me."

Oh! foolish one, these are falsehoods and delusions
That come from an illusory existence.

As your essence is nothingness,
How can you have Free-will?
Seeing that your being is one with not-being,
Whence comes this Free-will of yours?

Imagination distributes actions
As in a play or a farce,

For when your actions were planned,
Before your existence,
You were created for a certain purpose,
By the desire of the Truth.
Therefore is man predestined, before his existence,
To certain appointed work.
. . . (Oh, wondrous ways of Thine, without how or why!)

The honour of man consists of slavery,
In having no share of Free-will.

Of himself man has nothing,
Yet of good and evil God asks him,
Man has no choice, he is under control.
Oh! poor soul, he seems free, yet is a slave.

Give yourself up to the Truth,
For you are helpless in his grasp;
Freedom from self you will find in the All,
And, O Dervish! in the Truth you will find riches.

MAN: HIS CAPABILITIES AND HIS DESTINY

TO THE SŪFĪS

You are bound by a chord
To the soul of the creatures before you,
Therefore they are subject to your dominion,
And the soul of each is hidden in you.
In the midst of the world you are the kernel,
The centre of the world.
. . . The world of reason and mind is your fortune,
Earth and heavens your garments.
. . Your natural powers are ten thousand
Transcending limits and reckonings.

"I" AND "YOU"

"I" AND "you" are but the lattices,
In the niches of a lamp,
Through which the One Light shines.

"I" and "you" are the veil
Between heaven and earth;
Lift this veil and you will see
No longer the bond of sects and creeds.
When "I" and "you" do not exist,
What is mosque, what is synagogue?
What is the Temple of Fire?

REFLECTED FORMS OF HABIT

REPEAT an action several times
And you master it;
Habit makes dispositions
As fruits become ripe by time.
By practice man learns a trade,
By habit he collects his thoughts.
Remember at the last day
All your habits and actions
Will be clearly seen,
For the garment of the body
Will be stripped. And the form left
Will reflect your vices and virtues,
As objects are reflected in pure water.

Again, your dispositions will be embodied,
Made manifest as lights and fires;
For all phenomenal limitations will be removed.
You who are pure from earthly form,
Illumined by the Truth,
Will appear all heart,
From your stainless love.
Then will you be possessed by intoxication,
Scattering in confusion the two worlds.

THE LOWEST NECESSARY

IF there were no sweepers in the world
The world would be buried in dust.

A FAITHFUL SERVANT

To become a faithful servant,
Cultivate faith and sincerity,
Renew your belief every instant

While unbelief dwells in your heart.
Abandon the wish to be seen of men,
Cast off the blue-patched robe
Of the dervish
And bind on the Magian girdle.

Be a believer, be a believer, be a believer!

"FAR" AND "NEAR"

IF He sheds His Light on you,
You become near to Him
And far from your own existence.
For by nearness to Him

You become far from yourself.
What profit is there to you
In your non-existent existence?

THE SAGE

VIRTUE and equity,
Courage and temperance,
Are the four qualities of the sage.

He is not over-cunning or a fool,
His appetites are under control,
From cringing and boasting he is free,
And from foolhardiness and cowardice.
All virtues lie between
Excess and defect,
A narrow path betwixt
Hell's bottomless abyss,
Fine and sharp as a sword blade,
Which permits no lingering

Or turning round.

Equipoise is the summit of perfection,
Becoming like a simple essence.

As the rays of the sun
Shine upon the earth,
So the Light from the Spirit World
Shines brightly on him
Who has attained this equilibrium.

THE PROPHET AND THE SAINT

THE prophet, resplendent in his perfection,
Is as the sun's bright light,
And the saint, concealing his saintship,
Is as the subdued light of the moon.
By fellowship, the saint
Is intimate with the prophet,
And finding entrance to that secret chamber,
He loves and is beloved by the Truth.

THE FIRST AND THE LAST

THE two worlds produced the soul of Adam,
Which, though first in thought, was created last.

In man's self is disclosed the final cause,
For there is none beyond him.
O first, who are also the substance of the last!
O hidden, who are also the essence of the manifest!
You, who day and night are wondering about yourself,
Think of self no more,
For the end of such thought is confusion.

ANNIHILATION OF PHENOMENA

THE heavens and the stars
At the appointed time will disappear.
A wave will strike the earth,
And lo! it vanishes.

Only the Truth will remain Unchangeable.
And you at that moment,
Passing from this dream-life,
With self discarded,
Will be one with the Beloved.

Oh! Master, ponder on your coming and your going,
And the thousand existences that lie before you!

THE WRITTEN FAITH

READ the writing on your heart,
And you will understand whatever you desire,
For on the day he kneaded the clay,
He wrote on your heart, by grace, the faith.

THE PERFECT MAN

IN spite of his inheritance,
The perfect man is a slave
And does the work of a slave.
The law is his outer garment,
Though his inner is the mystic path.
He is famed for knowledge and devotion,
But he is far from all these,
For he is absorbed in the contemplation of the One.
. . . When his pilgrimage is over
He receives the crown of Khalifate.

THE ONE

THE NAME

EACH creature has its being
From the One Name,
From which it comes forth,
And to which it returns,
With praises unending.

THE BELOVED GUEST

CAST away your existence entirely,
For it is nought but weeds and refuse,
Go, clear out your heart's chamber,
Arrange it as the abiding-place of the Beloved.
When you go forth, He will come in,
And to you, with self discarded,
He will unveil His beauty.

THE SHADOWLESS

ON the narrow path of Truth,
On the Meridian line, He stands upright,
Throwing no shadow before or behind Him,
To the right hand or the left.
East and west is His Kibla cast,
Drowned in a blaze of radiant light.
Hail, O Light of God, O Shadowless Divinity!

THE UNKNOWABLE

PONDER on God's mercies,
But not on His essence.
For His works come forth from His essence,
Not His essence from His works.
His light shines on the whole universe,
Yet He Himself is hidden from the universe.

THE BOOK OF GOD

THE universe is God's book,
And he to whom the vision of the Divine

Has been vouchsafed
Reads therein and understands.
Substance is its consonants and accidents its vowels,
And different creatures are its signs and pauses.
The first verse is "Universal Reason,"
The second "Universal Soul," the "verse of light,"
And this is as a brightly shining lamp.
The third is the "Highest heavens,
The fourth "The Throne."
After there are seven transcendent spheres,
The "chapter of the seven limbs,"
And forms of the four elements,
Then Nature's three kingdoms
Whose verses none can count.
And last of all came down the soul of man.

THE UNCHANGING LIGHT

You fancy this world is permanent of itself
And endures because of its own nature,
But really it is a ray of light from the Truth

And within it the Truth is concealed.

And this light alters not nor varies
And is void of change or degree.
If the sun tarried always in one spot,
And ever shone in the same degree,
None would know that the light comes from him.

FUTURE REWARD

PONDER here and now on His qualities,
That you may behold Him Himself to-morrow.

THE SELF

THE GAMBLE OF THE SELF

REAL prayer can only be yours
When you have staked and gambled yourself away
And your essence is pure.
Then "a joy of the eyes" are your prayers
And no separation remains,
For knower and known are one and the same.

TRANSCEND SELF

RISE above time and space,
Pass by the world, and be to yourself your own world.

SELFLESSNESS

IN the empty heart, void of self
Can be heard the echoing cry,
"I am the Truth."
Thus is man one with the Eternal,
Travelling, travel and traveller have become one.

IDOLS, GIRDLES, AND CHRISTIANITY

ARE you still turning to great and small?
Pondering on religion and piety,
Teachership and discipleship?
Which mean hypocrisy and bondage.
Then idols and girdles
And Christianity are still yours.

IDOLS

THE idol's real being is not vain
Because God created it,
And all things from Him are good.
Being is pure good, if it contains evil
That comes from "other."
Truth is idol-worship,
If the Mussulman only knew;

But he sees in idols
Only the visible creature,
Not the Truth hidden in the idol.
Idol-worship is unification,
Since all things are the symbols of Being.

By counting beads, repeating prayers,
And reading the Koran,
The heathen becomes not a Mussulman.
The man to whom true infidelity becomes revealed
With pretended faith becomes disgusted.

Within every body a soul is hidden,
And true faith conceals infidelity.

Who adorned the face of the idol
With such beauty?
And who becomes an idol-worshipper
Unless God wills it?

In all things
See but One, say One, know One,

THE GIRDLE

THE mark of service
Is the knotted girdle.
So gird your loins, like a valiant man
With manliness.
Cast aside vain tales,
And mystic states and visions;
Dream not of lights,
Of marvels, of miracles,
For your miracles are contained
In worshipping the Truth;
All else is pride, conceit,
And illusion of existence.

CHRISTIANITY

I SEE the desire of Christianity
Is purification from self,
And liberty from bondage.

There is a sanctuary of the soul,
The blessed portal of unity,

The nest of the Eternal.
God's Spirit (Jesus),
Who proceeds from the blessed Spirit,
Taught this doctrine.

In you is placed a soul,
Which is a sample of this blessed Spirit.
Find release from humanity's carnal desire
And you will enter the Divine Life.
And he who is pure as the angels are
Will be carried up to the fourth heaven.

THE MOSQUE AND THE CLOISTER

IF "other" and "others" are before your eyes,
Then a mosque is no better
Than a Christian cloister;
But when the garment of "other" is cast off by you,
The cloister becomes a mosque.

THOUGHTS

CIRCLES

BEHOLD the world mingled together,
Angels with demons, Satan with the archangel.
All mingled like seed and fruit,
Infidel with faithful, and faithful with infidel.
At the point of the present are gathered
All cycles and seasons, day, month, and year.
World at beginning is world without end. [1]

... From every point in this circle
A thousand forms are drawn;
Every point as it revolves in a circle
Is now a circle, now a circling circumference.

DEATH

DEATH occurs to man in three ways:
First he dies every moment by his earthly nature;
Then, when his will perishes, he dies again;
And lastly at the separation of soul and body.

THE HEAVENS

LET not the prison of nature detain you,
But come forth and view the art of the Divine,
Contemplate the appearance of the heavens,

---

[1] There is no past or present with God, but an eternal Now.

So that praise and wonder for the Truth will be thine.

The arch of the high heavens enclosing both worlds
Is called "The Throne of the Merciful,"
And like the heart of man is ever moving,
Never resting for a moment.
Perchance man's heart is the central point
And heaven the circumference.

Within a day and a night
Heaven outspans your circuits, O dervish!

The other heavenly spheres are circling too,
Remember they all move in one direction,
From east to west like a water wheel,
Rushing on without food or sleep.

When the astrologer is an unbeliever,
He sees not that these circulating lights of heaven
Are dominated and controlled by The Truth.

NO COMPLETE HAPPINESS HERE

WHOM have you seen in the whole world
Who ever once acquired pleasure without pain?
Who, in attaining all his desires,
Has remained at his height of perfection?

THE ATOMS

TAKE one atom away from its place
And the whole world will fall to pieces;
The world is whirling dizzily, yet no one part
Moves from the limit of its place.
Each atom, held in bondage,

Despairs at its separation from the whole;
So though imprisoned, yet moves,

Though unclothed, yet is clothed again,
Though at rest, yet is always wandering,
Never beginning and never ending;
Each possessing self-knowledge, and so
Hurrying towards the throne on high.
Each atom hides beneath its veil
The soul-amazing beauty of the Beloved's Face.

THE PRAISE OF THE ATOMS

CONTINUALLY dwelling in all mystic lore,
Continually singing the song of praise
The atoms of the world will seem to you
Drunken and heavy with wine.

. . . When you have carded self
Like the wool-carder, you will raise a cry.
Oh! take the cotton of illusion from your ears,
And hearken to the call of the One, the Almighty.
. . . Why tarry till the last day
When now, in the valley of peace,
The very bush will say to you, "I am Allah"?

THINKING

THINKING is passing from the false to the true
And seeing the Absolute Whole in the part.
When the idea enters the mind,
It is a reminiscence of a former state,
And passes on to interpretation.

. . . He who sees by illumination
Discerns God first in everything,
But he who sees by logic only,
And seeks to prove the necessary,
Is bewildered and sometimes travels
Backward in a circle, or is imprisoned
In a chain of proofs.
Fool! he seeks the dazzling sun
By the dim light of a candle in the desert.

THOUGHTS ON CREATION

THE heavens revolve day and night
Like a potter's wheel,
And every moment the Master's wisdom
Creates a new vessel. For all that exists
Comes from one hand, one workshop.

Why do the stars set?
Going from perfection to defection?
Why do they change position,
Place, circuit, colour, and form?
Or why is heaven fretted by fire
Always whirling through desire?
Why are the planets revolving,
Above or beneath the earth?
The elements which are below the heavens
Serve in their appointed place
Ever united together.
From them is born the threefold
Kingdom of Nature;
Minerals, then plants and animals,
Waiting in their places as He wills.
Minerals, low in the dust, plants standing upright,
Animals, by their natural passions,

Preserving, continuing their races and species.

All, bowing to their Master's commands,
Fulfil His will day and night.

THE LIGHT MANIFEST

THE LIGHT

THE Light which is manifest
Leads all hearts captive,
Now as the minstrel, now as the cupbearer.

What a singer is He who, by one strain of sweet melody,
Burns the harvests of a hundred devotees!
What a cupbearer is He who, by a single goblet,
Inebriates two hundred threescore and ten!

Entering the Mosque at dawn,
He leaves there no wakeful man;
Entering the cloister at night,
He makes a fable of Sūfīs' tales;
Entering the college veiled as a drunkard,
The professor becomes hopelessly drunken.

Devotees go mad for love of Him
And become outcasts from house and home,
He makes one faithful, another an infidel,
Disturbing the world.
Taverns have been glorified by His lips,
Mosques have become shining by His cheek.

All I desire I have found in Him,
Gaining deliverance from self,
My heart was ignorant of itself,
Veiled from Him by a hundred veils

Of vanity, conceit, and illusion.

THE VISIT

ONE day at the dawn
The fair idol entered my door
And woke me from my sleep
Of slothful ignorance.
The secret chamber of my soul
Was illumined by His face,
And my being was revealed to me
In its true light.
I heaved a sigh of wonder
When I saw that fair face.
He spoke to me, saying,

"All thy life thou has sought
Name and fame;
This self-seeking of thine
Is an illusion, keeping thee back from Me.
To glance at My face for an instant
Is worth a thousand years of devotion."

Yes, the face of that world-adorner
Was shown unveiled before mine eyes;
My soul was darkened with shame
To remember my lost life,
My wasted days.

THE GIFT

THEN that moon
Whose face shone like the sun,
Seeing I had cast hope away,

Filled a goblet of Divine Knowledge
And, passing to me, bade me drink,
Saying, "With this wine,
Tasteless and odourless,
Wash away the writing
On thy being's tablet."

THE EFFECT OF THE DRAUGHT

INTOXICATED from the pure draught
Which I had drained to the dregs,
In the bare dust I fell.
Since then I know not if I exist or not,
But I am not sober, neither am I ill or drunken.
Sometimes, like His eye, I am full of joy,
Or, like His curl, I am waving;
Sometimes, alas! from habit or nature,
I am lying on a dust heap.
Sometimes, at a glance from Him,
I am back in the Rose Garden.

EPILOGUE

THIS bouquet of scented blossoms
I have plucked from that garden,
And have called it "The Secret Rose Garden."
In it are blooming
Roses of the mysteries of the heart
Untold before;
In it the tongues of the lilies are all singing,
And the eyes of the narcissus behold all, far and near.
Gaze on each one of these with your heart's eyes
Till your doubts melt away.
You will see tradition, earthly and mystical truths,
All arranged clearly in knowledge of detail.
Do not seek with cold eyes to find blemishes,
Or the roses will turn to thorns as you gaze.
Ingratitude is a sign of ignorance,
For those who know the truth are thankful.
When you remember me, breathe "Mercy be upon him."
I am ending with my own name,
"O Allah, grant me a 'Lauded' end." [1]

---

[1] I.e. Mahmud.

www.ingramcontent.com/pod-product-compliance
Lightning Source LLC
Chambersburg PA
CBHW051553010526
44118CB00022B/2688